Carole Boston Weatherford: THE CAROLINA PARAKEET

"*Perruche à tête jaune*" *from Dictionnaire*
Universel d'Histoire Naturelle, *1835-1844,*
by Charles D. d'Orbigny.
(Rare and Manuscript Collections,
Karl A Kroch Library, Cornell University)

THE CAROLINA PARAKEET
AMERICA'S LOST PARROT IN ART AND MEMORY

BY CAROLE BOSTON WEATHERFORD

Copyright © 2005 by Carole Boston Weatherford

Avian Publications
6380 Monroe St. NE
Minneapolis MN 55432

Bruce Burchett Publisher/Owner
www.avianpublications.com
bruce@avianpublications.com
Phone & fax 763-571-8902

All rights reserved. No part of this work covered by copyrights may be reproduced or used in any form or by any means, graphic, electronic or mechanical including photocopying, recording, taping or information storage or retrieval systems, without the prior written consent of the publisher.

ISBN 0-910335-01-X

Picture research was partially funded by a Central Piedmont Regional Artist Hub Grant from the North Carolina Arts Council.

Cover Art:
"La Perruche à l'ête jaune" by Jacques Barraband from Histoire naturelle de perroquets, vol. 1. *(Ernst Mayr Library of Comparative Zoology, Harvard university); and "Southern River Scenery" by Currier & Ives (Printed with permission of Travelers Property Casualty).*

Production and Design
Silvio Mattacchione and Co. / Peter A. Graziano Limited
1251 Scugog Line 8, RR#1.
Port Perry, ON, Canada L9L 1B2
Telephone: 905.985.3555
Fax: 905.985.4005
silvio@silvio-co.com
graziano@lincsat.com

www.silvio-co.com

Carolina Parrot from The Bird Book *by Chester A. Reed, 1914.*
(Courtesy of the Central Library System, University of Wisconsin-Madison)

Table of Contents

Introduction 8
List of Illustrations 7

CHAPTER ONE - Great Flocks
10
Explorers and naturalists marvel at the exotic bird.

CHAPTER TWO - A Real Ornament
22
The bird is sought after for its plumage and as a pet.

CHAPTER THREE - Marauding Mischiefs
34
An appetite for agricultural crops makes the bird a pest.

CHAPTER FOUR - Rare Birds
42
Over the span of a century, the great flocks dwindle.

CHAPTER FIVE - The Last Parakeet
50
In the wild and in captivity, the remaining birds perish.

CHAPTER SIX - A Perfect Likeness
56
The extinct bird captivates contemporary artists.

The Carolina Parakeet's Former Range 68
Museum Listing 70
Bibliography 75

List of Illustrations

Perruche · tête jaune (d'Orbigny)	2
Carolina Parrot (Reed)	5
La Perruche · tête jaune (Barraband)	9
Carolina Parakeet museum specimen	10
Southern River Scenery (Currier & Ives)	11
Native American fishing	11
Flock of passenger pigeons	12
Parrot of the Carolinas (Catesby)	13
Foot, wing, bill and tail of Carolina Parakeet	15
Carolina Parrot (Nuttall)	16
Carolina Parrot (Audubon)	17
Carolina Parrot (Wilson)	20
Bamboo canebrake	21
Carolina Parrot (Greene)	23
Carolina Parakeet egg	24
Feathers spark a fashion craze	27
The Young Oologist	28
Alexander Wilson	30
Birdcage	31
Carolina Parakeet (Baird)	35
Cypress Swamp, Illinois	36
American Fruit Piece (Currier & Ives)	37
John James Audubon	38
American Farm Life (Currier & Ives)	39
Carolina Parakeet (Audubon)	40
Carolina Parakeet (Studer)	42
European honeybee	43
The City of New Orleans (Currier & Ives)	44
The First Bird of the Season (Currier & Ives)	45
Carolina Parakeet specimens	47
Doodles, a pet Carolina Parakeet	48
Taylor Creek, Florida	49
Carolina Parakeet (Fuertes)	51
Young woman with pet parrot	52
Carolina Parrot (Wood)	53
Aviaries at Cincinnati Zoological Gardens	54
Santee Swamp, South Carolina	55
Live Carolina Parakeet	57
Carolina Parakeet (Gilliland)	58
Carolina Parakeet (Packard)	60
Carolina Parakeets (Hunter)	61
Carolina Parakeets (Hunter)	62
Carolina Parakeets and Orchids (Baggette)	63
Carolina Parakeets (McKoy)	65
Map of the species' former range	68
Carolina Parakeet (Larvalbug)	69

Introduction

We have seen no bird of the size, with plumage so brilliant. They impart a singular magnificence to the forest prospect, as they are seen darting through the foliage, and among the white branches of the sycamore.

*Timothy Flint in
The History and Geography of the Mississippi Valley,
1832*

Many early settlers and naturalists wrote of the Carolina Parakeet in journals, diaries and natural histories. However, the knowledge we inherited about the species from these firsthand accounts is sketchy and anecdotal. The mysteries of the Carolina Parakeet could fill a book. The bird's courtship behavior is undocumented, as are its nesting habits, breeding season and territory, incubation period, rate of reproduction and longevity in the wild. Though several museums possess eggs collected from captive Carolina Parakeets, not a single egg taken from the wild can be definitively categorized as that of a Carolina Parakeet.

These gaps are grievous, but understandable. The bird's green and gold plumage made it almost invisible amidst lush foliage in swamps, lowlands and deciduous riverbottom forests. And the birds roosted in hollows, hidden from the human eye. Ornithologists of the day were focused on collecting specimens rather than documenting life history and behavior. Thus, the species vanished from Earth before having been adequately researched.

This much is certain. There was once a gem in The Great Forest; a winged jewel rivaling any in the tropics. It was the Carolina Parakeet, North America's only native parrot. Curiously, within the span of a century, the great flocks dwindled to nothing, and this thing of beauty disappeared.

INTRODUCTION

Now, it is almost forgotten. All that remain are romantic tableaux penned by pioneers, likenesses limned by artists, specimens cataloged in collections, and longing, wistful longing.

This is the sobering story of how a young nation loved, laid waste and lost its only parrot.

"Le Perruche à tête jaune" by Jacques Barraband from
Histoire naturelle des perroquets, vol. 1.
(Ernst Mayr Library of the Museum of Comparative Zoology, Harvard University)

CHAPTER ONE

Great Flocks

In the Treasures Hall of the North Carolina Museum of Natural Sciences in Raleigh, visitors linger at a glass case atop a pedestal. Inside are Carolina Parakeets, stuffed birds with plumage so vivid that even the most jaded onlookers are awestruck. They ponder the specimens and read the accompanying description. Voices hush and the mood momentarily turns meditative. Then, youthful curiosity intervenes. "Does it still live in the forest?" a youngster chirps.

We wish. The Carolina Parakeet is extinct – a vanished breed. But once, it painted the wilderness.

When European explorers reached North America, nature rolled out the welcome mat. Bamboo canebrakes spanning hundreds of miles. Sycamore seven feet around. And sylvan forests so boundless that some colonists claimed a squirrel could scamper from Maine to Mississippi without ever leaving the canopy.

Rivers and bays offered a bounty. Lobsters sometimes weighed in at twenty pounds, and many Massachusetts oys-

Carolina Parakeet exhibit at Museum of Natural Science, Louisiana State University, Baton Rouge, Louisiana. (Photo by Mark S. Hafner)

CHAPTER ONE *Great Flocks*

*"Southern River Scenery" by Currier & Ives.
(Printed with permission of Travelers Property Casualty)*

ters had to be sliced in thirds to be swallowed. Whopping catches were common. Native Americans easily spotted and speared colossal fish: trout as long as a man's arm, catfish outweighing a woman, and sturgeon six to nine feet long. There was no need to concoct fish stories.

From the skies, massive flocks of passenger pigeons – sometimes billions of birds strong and hundreds of miles long – blotted out the sunlight

European explorers glimpsed Native Americans spearing whopping catches. (Treasures of the National Oceanic and Atmospheric Administration Library Collection)

Flocks of passenger pigeons – sometimes a billion birds strong – shadowed the land for hours as they passed overhead. Illustrated Sporting and Dramatic News, July 3, 1875. (Collection of Garrie Landry)

and shadowed the land for hours, as if an eclipse. The early settlers were amazed by the abundant wildfowl. On a 1585 expedition sponsored by Sir Walter Raleigh, Thomas Hariot observed several bird species, including "parats," on the Carolina coast.

Of a 1664 expedition, Commander William Hilton wrote, "We saw . . . in the woods . . . great flocks of parakeetos."

Colonial surveyor-general John Lawson also reported having seen "parrakeetos." While his contemporaries were flocking to Rome, Lawson impulsively ventured across the Atlantic after a passing acquaintance assured him that Carolina was the best country he could visit. Upon reaching North America in December 1700, Lawson embarked on a two-month, 550-mile portage from Charleston, South Carolina, to present-day Waxhaw, North Carolina. He then trekked across North Carolina, ending at present-day Beaufort County. After eight years of similar travels, Lawson deemed

CHAPTER ONE

Great Flocks

Carolina "as pleasant a country as any in Europe." In fact, he asserted that European flora and fauna paled in comparison to some American species. In his 1714 *Historie of Carolina*, Lawson ranked the parakeet among the American birds whose beauty surpassed those of Europe.

Hilton, Hariot and Lawson had seen the once plentiful Carolina Parakeet, the only parrot native to the North America. The bird's range extended from Florida to Virginia, west to Texas and Colorado, and north to Wisconsin.

Naturalist William Strachey's 1612 *The Historie of Travell into Virginia Britania* offered the first description of the species.

Parakitoes I haie seen many in the Winter and knowne divers killed, yet be they a Fowle most swift of wing, their winges and Breasts are of a greenish color with forked Tayles, their heades more Crymsen, some yellow, some orange-tawny, very beautyfull....

English naturalist Mark Catesby provided the first sci-

"Parrot of the Carolinas" by Mark Catesby, *from* The Natural History of Carolina, Florida and the Bahama Islands, *1731-1743. (North Carolina Collection. University of North Carolina Library at Chapel Hill)*

entific and illustrated account of the Carolina parakeet. Born in 1683 in Sudbury, England, Catesby – eager to study exotic American flora and fauna – joined his sister and brother-in-law in Virginia in 1712. He tramped hundreds of miles, mostly alone, fighting off disease and dodging warring Indians. During his expeditions, he collected and painted the plants and animals he observed. Concerned more with naturalistic accuracy than with artistic interpretation, he insisted upon painting only freshly picked plants and live animals. In a pioneering approach that foreshadowed the work of John James Audubon, Catesby's watercolors aimed to capture birds' peculiar gestures and to depict birds with the plants in their diets or natural habitats. Catesby preserved a few specimens in rum-filled jars and shipped them back to England. Sometimes, thirsty British sailors raided the specimen jars and drank the rum dry. In all, Catesby spent a decade in the American colonies documenting what he called "extraordinary curiosities of nature." He devoted another two decades to writing and publishing *The Natural History of Carolina, Florida, and the Bahama Islands* (1731-1743). While producing his magnum opus, he studied with a famed watercolorist and even learned to etch his own plates.

In a sentiment echoing Lawson, Catesby wrote, "The Birds of America generally excell those of Europe in the Beauty of their Plumage, but are much inferior to them in melodious notes." Catesby's hand-colored engraving, "The Parrot of Carolina," shows the bird eating cypress seeds. He noted not only the species' physique but also its uniqueness.

The bird is of the bigness, or rather less than a blackbird, weighing three ounces and a half; the fore part of the head orange color; the hind part of the head and neck yellow. All the rest of the bird appears green; but upon nearer scrutiny the interior vanes of most of the wing feathers are dark brown; the upper parts of the exterior vanes of the larger wing or quill feathers, are yellow, proceeding gradually deeper colored to the end, from yellow to green, and from green to blue; the edge of the shoulder of the wing, for

CHAPTER ONE   *Great Flocks*

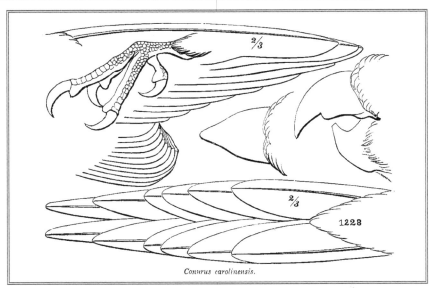

Foot, wing, bill and tail of Carolina Parakeet (A History of North American Birds: Land Birds, Vol. II, 1874, S. F. Baird, T. M. Brewer and R. Ridgway)

about three inches down, is bright orange color. The wings are very long as is the tail; having two middle feathers longer than the others by an inch and half, and end in a point; the rest are gradually shorter. The legs and feet are white; the small feathers covering the thighs, are green, ending at the knees with a verge of orange color. . . . This is the only one of the parrot kind in Carolina....

Measuring twelve inches from beak to tail, the Carolina Parakeet was the only species of the genus *Conuropsis*. In the 1758 edition of Linnaeus' *System Naturae*, the species was first given a scientific name. *Psittacus carolinensis* was a reference to Catesby's illustration "Parrot of Carolina." There were two distinct geographic races or subspecies of the bird: the true Carolina Parakeet *(Conuropsis carolinensis)* and the so-called Louisiana Parakeet *(Conuropsis ludovicianus)*. The nominate species, *carolinensis*, was common to the southeastern United States, The subspecies, *ludovicianus*, covered the rest of the bird's range throughout the Mississippi-Missouri basin in the eastern interior of the United States. The western subspecies was usually paler with bluish green – rather than greenish yellow – on the back and rump and also had more yellow on the wings.

Lewis and Clark's Corps of Discovery, which set out in 1803 to find a Northwest Passage, produced the first documented sighting of the bird west of the Mississippi. In a June 26, 1804 journal entry, explorer Meriwether Lewis mentioned that he had "observed a great number of Parrot queets" near the mouth of the Kansas River. On a similar expedition to the Louisiana Purchase territory, explorer Peter Custis noted, "Paroquets very numerous. They are always large flocks."

British botanist Thomas Nuttall studied North America's wildfowl during several botanical explorations. Born in 1786 in Yorkshire, England, Nuttall became a printer's apprentice in 1800. An interest in botany, however, enticed him to set sail for the Americas. The twenty-two-year-old began his career in botany just one day after his arrival in Philadelphia in 1808. A protégé of Benjamin Smith Barton, Nuttall was perhaps the most adventurous of the early American naturalists. Over the course of four decades, he explored the Great Lakes, Midwest, Pacific Northwest, Southeast and Middle Atlantic regions, collecting botanical and ornithological specimens along the way. Nuttall was also skilled as a printer, which is apparent in the woodblock prints that he created for *A Manual of the Ornithology of*

"Carolina Parrot" by Thomas Nuttall
(A Manual of the Ornithology of the United States and Canada: The Land Birds, 1814)

CHAPTER ONE   *Great Flocks*

"Carolina Parrot" by John James Audubon. (pfMS Am 21(88) by permission of Houghton Library, Harvard University)

the United States and Canada: The Land Birds.

In the 1832 volume, the first American handbook of birds, Nuttall described the Carolina Parakeet's habitat and behavior.

The Carolina Parrakeets in all their movements, which are uniformly gregarious, show a peculiar predilection for the alluvial, rich, and dark forests bordering the principal rivers and larger streams, in which the towering cypress and gigantic sycamore spread their vast summits, or stretch their innumerable arms, over a wide waste of moving or stagnant waters. . . . The flocks, . . . dart in swift and airy phalanx through the green boughs of the forest; screaming in general concert, they wheel in wide and descending circles round the tall button-wood, and alight in the same instant, their green vesture like the fairy mantle, rendering them nearly invisible beneath the shady branches, where they sit, perhaps, arranging their plumage, and shuffling side by side, seem to caress, and scratch each other's heads with all the fondness and unvarying friendship of affectionate Doves.

Flocks, numbering a dozen to the hundreds, flew in small, tight formations, squawking constantly as they snaked through the sky. On expeditions along the Mississippi and Missouri rivers, naturalist and wildlife artist John James Audubon witnessed flocks in abundance. In 1820 in his *Mississippi River Journal*, he wrote, "the woods literally filled with Parokeets;" "Immense flocks. . . ." Near Mobile, Alabama, in 1837, he saw "Parokeets by the hundreds." And during his last field trip – an 1843 expedition up the Missouri River – Audubon noted, "Parrakeets . . . plentiful. . . ." These multitudes belied the fact that early writers' musings would become the bird's epitaph.

The Carolina Parakeet thrived in heavily timbered lowlands, swamps and riversides. As Nuttall noted, the green and gold birds were hardly visible in lush green foliage of cypress swamps, bamboo canebrakes and deciduous bottomwood forests. But when the bird emerged from the leaves, the early settlers glimpsed paradise; a flash of the tropics in sea green, lemon, lime, tangerine, and sky-blue hues. "It is a pleasant sight to see a flock of them suddenly wheel in the atmosphere, and light upon a tree; their gaudy colors are reflected in the sun with the brilliance of a rainbow," wrote H. R. Schoolcraft in an 1819 list of Missouri birds .

CHAPTER ONE

In Charles Bendire's 1892 government-commissioned volume, *Life Histories of North American Birds*, E. A., McIlhenny noted the birds' agility.

The flight of the Carolina Paroquet, once seen, is never to be forgotten. Their flight which is more or less undulating . . . is extremely swift and graceful, enabling them, even when flying in rather compact flocks, to dart in and out of the densest timber with ease.

Alexander Wilson, the father of American ornithology, also beheld the Carolina Parakeet in flight. In his 1814 publication, *American Ornithology*, Wilson wrote:

They fly... in close, compact bodies, and with great rapidity, making a loud and outrageous screaming.... Their flight is sometimes in a direct line; but most usually circuitous, making a great variety of elegant and serpentine meanders, as if for pleasure.

Audubon observed a more deliberate flight pattern: rapid and straight, deviating from a direct course only to avoid obstacles. According to Audubon, when a flock of parakeets reached a feeding area, they did not alight immediately. Instead, they surveyed the area, circling repeatedly and gradually lowering until they almost touched the ground. Then, they suddenly re-ascended and landed all at once on the fruit tree or on a tree near the field that they intended to plunder. If disturbed from their perch, one bird would utter a shrill cry, signalling the flock to take wing instantaneously and in unison.

Though observers extolled the parakeet's plumage, they had no such praise for its raucous, discordant voice. "Their call notes are shrill and disagreeable, a kind of grating, metallic shriek," wrote Bendire. In flight, the flocks yelled continually, "qui, qui, qui-i-i-i."

Nineteenth century naturalist C. J. Maynard noted, "The parakeets scream very loudly when flying; so loudly, in fact that their shrill cries can be heard for miles." The bird also shrieked when startled.

However, the bird's tenor was markedly different when perched or feeding. Carolina Parakeets gossiped intermittently in a low mumble.

"Carolina Parrot" (top) by Alexander Wilson from American Ornithology, 1814.
(American Philosophical Society)

Bendire observed:

When at rest in the middle of the day on some favorite tree, they sometimes utter low notes, as if talking to each other, but more often they remain entirely silent, and are then extremely difficult to discover as their plumage harmonizes and blends thoroughly with the surrounding plumage.

gathered in small bands atop the tallest trees, chattering all the while. At sunrise, they flew to the nearest mulberry grove. There, the noisy birds fed from sunrise to 7 a.m. and again from 5 p.m. to sunset. After the morning feeding, they went to the nearest stream to drink and bathe.

Lush foliage of bamboo canebrakes camouflaged the Caralina Parakeet.

E. A. McIlhenny, who encountered Carolina Parakeets in southern Louisiana, reported the bird's daily habits to Bendire. In the morning just before sunrise, the parakeets

"They spent the rest of the day and roosted at night in live-oak timber," McIlhenny reported. 🐦

CHAPTER TWO

A Real Ornament

Though graceful in flight, the Carolina Parakeet was slow and awkward on foot. The birds were so slow on the ground that people could sometimes approach them. Wilson described the bird's gait as "lame and crawling." This clumsiness did not make the bird any less captivating, however. Ornithologist Alexander Wilson observed:

When they alighted on the ground, it appeared, at a distance, as if covered with a carpet of the richest green, orange and yellow. They afterwards settled, in one body, on a neighboring tree, which stood detached from any other, covering almost every twig of it, and the sun shining strongly on their gay and glossy plumage, produced a very beautiful and splendid appearance.

Just as flocks carpeted the ground, they emblazoned bare trees. Using its hooked bill to grip, the Carolina Parakeet scrambled up tree trunks and moved nimbly on tree limbs. Right side up or upside down, the birds clambered from limb to limb as if acrobats – a wondrous spectacle indeed. Often, the birds scratched each other's heads and necks. The birds roosted in groups of thirty to forty in the hollows of trees, such as cypress and sycamore, and in holes left by large woodpeckers. At night, they nestled close to each other, sometimes in a perpendicular position, supported by bills and claws.

There is no documented evidence of a parakeet's nest, leading author of *Hope Is The Thing With Feathers: A Personal Chronicle of Vanished Birds*, Christopher Cokinos, to conclude that no one ever saw one. Conflicting accounts state that groups of parakeets laid their eggs together in holes of trees or in fragile nests made from twigs in tree forks. Writing in 1889, William

CHAPTER TWO   *A Real Ornament*

Carolina Parrot, from Parrots in Captivity, *1884-1887, by W. T. Greene.
(Rare and Manuscripts Collections, Karl A. Kroch Library, Cornell University)*

Brewster shared secondhand accounts gleaned during a Florida trip. Brewster reported that a Judge R. L. Long of Tallahassee corroborated the accounts of two hunters who described the nests "as flimsy structures built of twigs and placed on the branches of cypress trees." Two young parakeets were taken from one such nest. When the birds were abundant in the region, Long had found them breeding in large colonies – some a thousand birds strong – in the cypress swamps.

Charles Bendire concluded that the sociable Carolina Parakeet may have resorted to open nesting sites because sufficient, suitable tree cavities were rarely found in close proximity.

The female birds probably laid one to four (usually two) round, light-greenish, white unspotted eggs at a time. Many females laid their eggs together. The length of incubation is undocumented. And it is unknown whether the male or female of the species incubated the eggs. The new hatchlings were altrical. They stayed in the nest for a relatively long time and were cared for by adults. The young fledged eighteen-to-nineteen days after hatching. During the bird's first season, grayish or brownish down was replaced by solid green feathers. By age two, the adult birds achieved their full plumage. The bird's breeding habits remain a mystery.

Egg taken from a Carolina Parakeet in captivity, from The Bird Book, *1914, by Chester A. Reed. (Courtesy of the Central Library System, University of Wisconsin-Madison)*

Early settlers did surmise that the Carolina Parakeet did not fly south for the winter. "In winter there are great plenty of Parrats," Captain John Smith wrote of Virginia. Thomas Nuttall stated that the birds appeared in St. Louis, Missouri, in the dead of winter. Alexander Wilson saw a flock on the Ohio River during a snowstorm. In 1790, ornithologist Benjamin Smith Barton wrote that a January sighting of a flock northwest of Albany, New York, alarmed Dutch settlers who regarded the birds' unseasonable advent as an evil omen. This non-migratory lifestyle was a consequence of the bird's vigor and varied diet.

While some pioneers were amazed that this tropical-looking creature endured snow and below-freezing temperatures, preeminent botanist William Bartram found the bird's hardiness implausible. Shortly after the American Revolution, he wrote:

I was assured in Carolina that these birds, for a month or two in the coldest winter weather, house themselves in hollow Cypress trees, clinging fast to each other like bees in a hive, where they continue in a torpid state until the warmth of the returning spring reanimates them, when they issue forth from their late dark, cold winter cloisters. But I have lived several years in North Carolina and never was witness to an instance of it, yet I do not at all doubt but that there have been instances of belated flocks thus surprised by sudden severe cold and forced into such shelter, and the extraordinary severity and perseverance of the season might have benumbed them into a torpid, sleepy state; but that they all willingly should yield to so disagreeable and hazardous a situation, does not seem reasonable or natural, when we consider that they are a bird of the swiftest flight and impatient of severe cold.

Flying in the face of skeptics such as Bartram, the Carolina Parakeet weathered the cold. A winter sighting of flocks in sycamores reminded Gert Goebel, a German settler in Missouri, of the young birch trees that Germans decorated at Christmas. The scene inspired this eloquent tribute in Goebel's 1877 autobiography:

These flocks of paroquets were a real ornament in the trees stripped of their foliage in winter. Their sight was particularly attractive, when such a flock of several hundred had settled on a big sycamore, when the bright green color of the birds was in such marked contrast with the white bark of the trees, and when the sun shone brightly upon these inhabited tree tops, the many yellow heads looked like so many candles.

This sight always reminded me vividly of a kind of Christmas tree which was used by the poorer families... only these enormous Christmas trees of the forest looked vastly more imposing than the little birch in the warm room.

Little wonder, then, that Native Americans used the bird's brilliant plumes for ornament. Much to the species' detriment, milliners and dressmakers also prized the Carolina Parakeet's luminous plumage. The feathers, and often dead birds, adorned women's hair, hats and gowns. Men also donned fedoras with feather trim. During two strolls in Manhattan in 1886, ornithologist Frank Chapman of the American Museum of Natural History spotted feathers from forty native bird species on 525 woman's hats. That year alone, the lavish fad claimed an estimated five million birds. By the turn of the century, hunters fetched $32 per ounce for plumes. Though parakeet plumes were not the most coveted – heron aigrettes held that hapless title – the hat trade nevertheless thinned Carolina Parakeet flocks.

Natural history collectors, seeking rarities for curiosity cabinets, also snatched up specimens: stuffed birds, skins and eggs. In the late nineteenth century, egg collecting – known as oology – became a national craze among scientists and hobbyists. A half dozen or so magazines were devoted to egg buying, trading and collecting. T. Gilbert Pearson, president of the Audubon Society from 1911 to 1937, was an avid egg collector as a youth. He shared this interest with boyhood friend Altie Quaintance. Together, the two boys, hunted, gathered and blew eggs. They exchanged eggs with each other and with collectors from afar.

In his autobiography, Pearson described this consuming passion. "We talked of eggs and we dreamed about them. We admired each other's eggs and quarreled about eggs. For months our lives were absorbed in the subject . . . ."

Countless Carolina Parakeet eggs were claimed by collectors. Further, ornithologists took eggs and shot birds in the wild

Woman with artificial birds adorning her hat and dress, c. 1902.
At the height of the feather fad, those birds might have been real.
(Library of Congress)

CHAPTER TWO *A Real Ornament*

Vol. 1. No. 12. GAINES, N. Y., APRIL, 1885. { PUBLISHED MONTHLY 60C. PER YEAR.

THE YOUNG OOLOGIST

EDITED AND PUBLISHED MONTHLY
— BY —
FRANK H. LATTIN,   GAINES, N. Y.

Printed by J. P. SMITH, 80 State St., Rochester, N.Y.

Correspondence and items of interest to the student of Birds, their Nests and Eggs solicited from all.

Terms of Subscription.

Single Subscription   -   -   60 cents per annum.
Foreign Countries,   -   -   - 75   "   "
Sample Copies,   -   -   -   -   6 cents each.
The above rates include postage.

Terms of Advertising,

Made known upon application. Send copy for estimate.

Remittances should be made by draft on New York; money order or postal note payable at Gaines, N. Y.; or by registered letter. Unused U. S. postage stamps of any denomination will be accepted for sums under one dollar. Address all subscriptions and communications to THE YOUNG OOLOGIST,
GAINES, Orleans Co., N. Y.
☞ Make money orders and drafts payable to
FRANK H. LATTIN.

Entered at the Post Office at Gaines, N. Y., as Second-class mail matter.

JOTTINGS.

We have compiled an exhaustive index for Vol. 1 of the YOUNG OOLOGIST. Never has there been published one-half the amount of valuable information for the collector at double the money as we have given our readers during the past year in our little monthly. We can, during the month of April, furnish Vol. I. complete —see index for contents—for only sixty cents. Complete your files while you can. Back numbers will soon be exceedingly rare and valuable and possibly not obtainable at any price.

SPECIAL NOTICE.—Each Number of Vol. II, of THE YOUNG OOLOGIST will contain 32 Pages. Subscriptions and Renewals will be received until April 20th, 1885, at 75 Cents. After that date $1.00. New Subscriptions can commence with any number.

The Knights of Audubon promises to be a great success. Several Legions have already been formed.

Look out for Eggs of the Owl, Hawk. Crow and other large species this month. It's now too late for many Owl's nests.

Hundreds of subscriptions expire with this issue. Renew at once. We cannot afford to lose a single subscriber.

During the month of April we shall open an office in Albion, and will then be able to attend to all correspondence the day received.

Oldroyd's inks are good enough for us. We are using gallons of them. A pint of any color costs only fifteen cents and we find it gives better satisfaction than the little bottles purchased at the stores for the same amount.

For our own benefit we have postponed the awarding of March prizes and have extended the time for closing the competition until April 20th, at which date the last subscriptions can be sent at 75c. This may possibly be our last competition.

for study. Yet, for all the nineteenth century collecting, only twelve sets of Carolina Parakeet eggs exist in North American museums today.

There was also a demand for live specimens. "They are often taken alive" wrote Colonial Surveyor - General John Lawson, "and become familiar and tame in two days." The exotic Carolina Parakeet was a popular and amusing pet. Despite the fact that it neither mimicked human speech nor sang sweetly, caged birds adorned parlors and porches. Parrots are among the smartest birds, perhaps as intelligent as chimpanzees and dolphins. Consequently, the Carolina Parakeet – though capable of inflicting a severe bite when wounded or held – adjusted quickly to captivity. A seemingly cruel practice – repeated plunges in water – was employed to tame wild parakeets. The captive birds ate soon after confinement.

Botanist Thomas Nuttall wrote: "The Carolina Parakeet is readily tamed, and early shows an attachment to those around who bestow any attention on its wants... As a domestic, [it] is very peaceable and rather taciturn."

Ornithologist Wilson wounded a Carolina Parakeet and kept it as a pet. He named it Poll. Using sticks, Wilson made a cage for the bird. Poll gnawed the sticks, repeatedly leaving portholes in the cage. Wilson carried Poll more than a thousand miles through the forest in a knotted silk handkerchief in his pocket. Along the way, he proceeded to train the bird. The pet bird learned its name and to respond when called. It climbed up Wilson's clothes, perched on his shoulder and ate from his mouth. At the campsite, the bird gazed into the fire, dozing from night till morning. The bird – which the Chickasaw and Choctaw knew as "kelinky" and the Seminoles called "puzzi la nee" or "pot pot chee" (Snyder, 1) – helped Wilson get acquainted with the Native Americans. For all the attention it garnered from Native American children, the caged bird must have longed for avian society, for a comrade of its own kind.

Below Natchez, Mississippi, Wilson bought a cage and placed it on a piazza. Poll's

Nineteenth century collectors subscribed to The Young Oologist *to buy and trade eggs.*

Alexander Wilson, the father of American ornithology, took a Carolina Parakeet as a pet. Portrait attributed to Thomas Sully. (American Philosophical Society)

call soon attracted passing flocks, which landed in nearby trees and conversed with the caged bird. Wilson slightly wounded one bird's wing, so the bird would stay. Poll quickly became attached to the wild bird. Wilson wrote:

The pleasure Poll expressed on meeting with this new companion was really amusing. She crept close up to it, as it hung on the side of the cage, chattered to it in a low tone of voice, as if sympathizing with its misfortune, scratched about its head and neck with her bill; and both at night nestled as close as possible to each other, sometimes Poll's head being thrust among the plumage of the other. On the death of this companion, she appeared restless and inconsolable for several days. On reaching New Orleans, I placed a looking-glass beside the place where she usually sat, and the instant she perceived her own image, all her former fondness seemed to return, so that she could scarcely absent herself from it a moment. It was evident she was completely deceived. Always when evening drew on, and often during the day, she laid her head close to that of the image in the glass, and began to doze with great composure and satisfaction.

Shortly thereafter, Wilson's experiment and Poll's initiation ended. Wilson took the bird with him to sea, and while he slept, the poor bird escaped from its cage and perished in the Gulf of Mexico.

Carolina Parakeets were sold as pets both in North America and Europe. In 1878, a Dr. Nowotny purchased a pair of the birds in Vienna. The birds were amusing, Nowotny wrote.

They were very fond of music. When my wife places the zither table near the cage in the evening, lights the lamp and begins to play, then rejoicing, headraising, bowing and wing beating takes place without measure. Similar pleasure was expressed . . . when we lit the Christmas tree. . . . They stand cold very well, but enjoy having their under parts touched by warm breath, for which purpose they cling to the wires and permit me to breath[sic] upon them, pecking me on the nose tenderly at the same time. In the cage I can play with them as I wish and even take them in my hands, but I dare not grasp or close hand, for then they slip away at once, screaming.

In 1879, Nowotny's birds bred, producing ten eggs and three hatchlings. Within six, weeks, however, the young birds had died. Unfortunately, the Carolina Parakeet seldom bred successfully in captivity. Frivolous ninteenth century aviculturists failed to see the imperative for captive breeding. They delighted in pet parakeets, but did not provide a diet or create an environment conducive to reproduction. Some parakeet eggs were destroyed by careless pet owners or by the birds themselves. Other times, the domesticated birds did not incubate the eggs or neglected the hatchlings.

On her parrot website, Shelly Lane laments the missed opportunity. "Because of its commonness and low price, it was not taken seriously by breeders . . . and basically was not domestically bred," Lane wrote. "Even a few breeding pairs could have kept this species alive, and perhaps could have restored it to the wild in time."

CHAPTER THREE

Marauding Mischiefs

In the wild, the Carolina Parakeet fed on seeds. It favored the seeds of the cocklebur, a prickly plant that often stuck to sheep's fleece. The bird, using its foot and curved beak, could unhusk seeds from a burr in the blink of an eye. The bird also ate nuts, berries, pawpaws, wild grapes, leaf buds and the seeds of the maple, elm, pine and cypress. The bald cypress fruit – a hard, pear-shaped cone – becomes woody when mature. Because few animals can open the tough fruit, most cones fall to the ground beneath the parent tree – denying the seedling necessary sunlight. With a hooked bill powerful enough to crack open the cones, the Carolina Parakeet was vital to the long-distance dissemination of the trees. Droppings from roving flocks spread the trees' seeds far beyond the swamps, sowing cypress in unlikely eastern piedmont regions.

The Carolina Parakeet ate sand and gravel to aid in digestion. Apparently dependent on salt, the bird drank salt water and rolled and scratched itself in the sand. Flocks of hundreds to thousands could be spotted around salt licks in the Midwest.

When the colonists carved fields, orchards and vineyards from the wilderness, the bird's diet grew more varied as it adopted new food sources. Botanist William Bartram recorded in his *Travels* that in North Carolina, the parakeet is "very numerous and we abound in all the fruits which they delight in."

Surveryor William Byrd described the bird in the early 1700s. "They are very Beautiful, but like some other pretty Creatures, they are apt to be loud and mischievous."

Colonial Surveyor - General John Lawson concurred "They are mischievous to orchards. They visit first, when Mulberries are ripe, which fruit

CHAPTER THREE   *Maurauding Mischiefs*

*Carolina Parakeet (*A History of North American Birds: Land Birds, Vol. II, *1874, by S. F. Baird, T. M. Brewer and R. Ridgway)*

The roving Carolina Parakeet, which ate bald cypress fruit, helped sow the tree's seeds far beyond the coastal plains.
(Cypress Swamp at Creek National Wildlife Refuge, Illinois; U.S. Fish and Wildlife Service)

they love extremely. They peck Apples, to eat the kernels, so that the Fruit rots and perishes." Much to farmers' dismay, the birds feasted on seeds and kernels of fruit. Marauding flocks swarmed orchards before the fruits ripened. Landing on a single tree, a flock quickly pecked apart small peaches, pears or apples to pluck out only the seeds. Bellies full, the birds flew off, leaving the ruined fruit to rot on the ground. Similarly, the birds gobbled stacks of grain put up in fields.

Ornithologist Alexanter Wilson observed, "I have known a flock of these birds alight on an apple tree, and have myself seen them twist off the fruit, one by one, strewing it in every direction around the tree, without observing that any of the depredators descended to pick them up."

Farmers abhorred this wanton destruction and viewed the birds as wasteful foragers. To protect the crops, farmers shot the birds. The Carolina Parakeet was an easy target. A flock would not abandon a wounded comrade and fly to safety. Instead, the shrieking flock swooped around the injured bird, likely a defensive tactic to chase the danger away. The more shots and fatalities, the greater the concern and commotion among the flock. Thus, gunfire continued until the whole hovering flock lay dead. Wilson noted:

At each successive discharge, though showers of them fell, yet the affection of the survivors seemed to increase; for after a few circuits around the place, they again alighted near me, looking down on their slaughtered companions with such manifest symptoms of sympathy and concern as entirely disarmed me.

Audubon also observed this group solidarity.

The gun is kept at work; eight or ten or even twenty, are killed at every discharge. I have seen several hundreds destroyed in this manner in the course of a few hours, and have procured a basketful of these birds at a few

Carolina Parakeets pecked apart fruit to pluck out only the seeds..
("American Fruit Piece" by Currier & Ives; Library of Congress)

CHAPTER THREE   *Maurauding Mischiefs*

*When early settlers carved forests into farm,
Carolina Parakeets feasted on grain and kernels of fruit.
("American Farm Life" by Currier & Ives; Library of Congress)*

shots, in order to make choice of good specimens for drawing...

Despite a tender heart, the creature had a destructive nature, Audubon surmised. "Nature seems to have implanted in these birds a propensity to destroy, in consequence of which they cut to atoms pieces of wood, books, and, in short, everything that comes their way."

The punishment may have outweighed the crime, however. Researchers have been hard-pressed to find a farmers' almanac or agricultural history that declared the bird a scourge to crops. In the end, more birds may have been shot for sport than for revenge.

Though the bird was regarded by many as a pestilence, Audubon admired the Carolina Parakeet, nevertheless. He saw the bird's beauty as proof of the woodland's delights.

Naturalist and wildlife artist John James Audubon painted the Carolina Parakeet around 1825. (Johnson, Fry & Co., 1861; American Philosophical Society)

Carole Boston Weatherford: THE CAROLINA PARAKEET

"Carolina Parakeet" by John James Audubon from
Birds of America, 1828-1830.
(North Carolina Collection, University of North Carolina Library
at Chapel Hill)

CHAPTER THREE   *Maurauding Mischiefs*

He wrote:

"The woods are the habitation best fitted for them, and there the richness of their plumage, their beautiful mode of flight, and even their screams, afford welcome intimation that our darkest forests and most sequestered swamps are not destitute of charms."

Around 1825, Audubon painted the Carolina Parakeet. By then, the bird was becoming scarce. "Our Parakeets are very rapidly diminishing in number;" the artist noted, "and in some districts, where twenty-five years ago they were plentiful, scarcely any are now to be seen." 🌍

CHAPTER FOUR

Rare Birds

Carolina Parakeet (Studer's Popular Ornithology, 1903, by Jacob Studer)

Most Americans took for granted that this exquisite creature would always exist. They could not have been more deluded. By 1850, the birds were seldom seen in the Carolinas and had almost disappeared in Georgia. After 1870, the rare sightings were of small flocks. In the 1890s, the breed's last stand was in remote Florida swamps. In 1889 – the same year a man reportedly shot two hundred birds in an orange grove – ornithologist W. E. D. Scott wrote:

With the settlement of the State this species has gradually disap-

peared till at the present time it must be regarded as a rare bird, though once so abundant and conspicuous . . . . The Paroquet seems to be one of the species that . . . disappears from settled regions, and it would seem to be a question of only a few years when Paroquets will be as unknown in most parts of Florida as they are in some of the states where the early settlers found them an abundant species.

By the end of the nineteenth century the Carolina Parakeet had nearly been wiped out. Slaughter hastened, but was not the sole cause of, the species' decline. As civilization encroached, the bird's habitat gradually disappeared. European honey bees – which Native Americans called "the white man's flies" – buzzed across North America, taking over hollows of trees for their hives. At the same time, bee hunters destroyed hollow trees for honey and wax. The dual threat of bees and bees culture may have disturbed flocks' nesting and roosting, biologist Daniel McKinley, the foremost authority on the species, suggests.

McKinley also suggests that the species' courtship and breeding rituals may have been induced, and its reproduction limited, by dependence on a nonannual environmental stimulus such as bamboo's seed production. Breeding may have been interrupted and nesting disturbed when settlers razed bamboo and cypress.

Though the Carolina Parakeet's diet was flexible, the bird may not have adapted as readily to changes in the natural environment. Ultimately, rapid loss of habitat may have sounded the death knell for the species. Within two centuries of the colonists' arrival in the eastern United States, about 162 million acres or one-quarter of the region's original forests had disappeared. Early American towns and plantations first

Hives of European honeybees may have displaced Carolina Parakeets from their homes in hollows of trees.

sprang up along rivers. The colonists destroyed forests for settlements and felled trees for timber and fuel. The cleared lands encompassed most of the eastern riverbottom forests – the Carolina Parakeet's habitat.

reduced the wild population. Professional trappers caught whole flocks at once by putting nets over entrance and exit holes of the hollow trees where the birds roosted. Trappers also netted flocks by using a

Early American cities, built along rivers, destroyed the Carolina Parakeet's habitat. ("The City of New Orleans" by Currier & Ives, c. 1885, Library of Congress)

Audubon apparently dreaded the effect of deforestation on wildlife. "When I see settlers cutting down the forest trees to make way for towns and farms," he wrote, "I pause and wonder."

Even as the species declined, the killing and capture of Carolina Parakeets went on. Farmers continued to take aim, the hat trade took a heavy toll, and the pet trade further

crippled bird as a lure. In Jacob Studer's 1881 natural history *The Birds of North America*, a Mr. Allen reported: "Hundreds are captured every winter on the Lower St. Johns [Florida] by professional bird catchers and sent to northern cities. Thousands of others are destroyed wantonly by sportsmen."

The bird's habit of gathering hardly made it fair game.

CHAPTER FOUR   *Rare Birds*

Within rifle range, the Carolina Parakeet never had a sporting chance. The bird also found its way into American cuisine. The flesh of young parakeets was pleasing to some palates. "A dozen of them make a most delicious sea-pie," wrote Christian Schultz in 1810. ". . . [T]he Parrakeet formerly inhabited large portions of the United States where it is now never seen," a Mr. Allen reported, "and the cause of its disappearance has been deemed a mystery."

This mystery still vexes experts. As recently as 1990, environmental historian Mikko Saikku theorized that a sequence of ultimate and proximate causes led to the Carolina Parakeet's extinction. He suspects habitat destruction was the ultimate cause that permitted proximate causes, such as hunting, the hat trade and pet trade, to ravage the species' wild population. Once the bird's numbers plummeted, this highly social species seemed unable to maintain itself, dooming it to extinction. With habitat destroyed and flocks thinning,

The Carolina Parakeet was easy prey for hunters.
("The First Bird of the Season," Currier & Ives, c. 1879, Library of Congress)

the Carolina Parakeet may have become so dispersed that it no longer reaped "the advantages of social nesting. . . to encourage a breeding rate higher than that of mortality," suggests Saikku.

In "Carolina Parakeet," a publication in *The Birds of North America* series, Noel F. Snyder and Keith Russell suggest that the bird's highly social nature and its tendency to feed near and roost in human structures made it vulnerable to diseases spread by poultry and livestock. Thus, Snyder and Russell suspect that disease may have exterminated the last flocks.

We will never know which factors dealt the worst blow. And we can only guess how climactic any single event was in the bird's disappearance. One thing is certain, however. All rivers of responsibility flowed from the same source – European settlers. They imported honeybees, cleared forests, drained swamps, shot birds, collected specimens, kept pet birds and donned feathered adornments. Over time, these combined forces decimated Carolina Parakeet populations throughout the bird's former range. The species was plunged into precipitous decline and sacrificed for short-term gains; a casualty of Manifest Destiny.

Sadly, the lesson in population dynamics was not readily grasped. In a perilous downward spiral, the species' rarity sparked rampant collecting. In the post-Civil War era, bird collecting was all the rage. And the Carolina Parakeet was wanted – dead or alive. Even ornithologists had blood on their hands, pursuing specimen collection rather than preservation of the species in the wild. Nineteenth century ornithologists did not rely on binoculars or field guides to identify birds. Instead, they shot the bird for later examination; a method that was, in their opinion, justified by science. In *A Passion for Birds*, Marvin Barrow, Jr. explains, "The ornithological community as a whole sought to protect birds while asserting the absolute right to collect them." In a 1985 census of museum collections worldwide, Biologist McKinley found more than eight hundred parakeet specimens – most collected in Florida in the latter half of the nineteenth century. Ultimately, scientific collecting drove one more nail in the species' coffin.

Collectors of the day were both shameless and greedy. In a letter about his Florida studies, ornithologist Robert Ridgway wrote, "I secured 26 specimens from a single flock, besides three others which being only slightly wounded, I brought home and kept in captivity for several years."

After Ridgway's pet parakeets produced offspring, he gave his friend, fellow bird lover Paul Bartsch, a hatchling that the parent birds were neglecting. Bartsch named the bird Doodles and nursed it to health. Doodles flitted around the house, played marbles, perched in the dining room window, had its own plate at meal time, napped with Bartsch, and even ate from his mouth. When the bird died in 1914, it was among the last of its kind.

Though no one knows exactly when or where the last Carolina Parakeet was taken in the wild, respected ornithologist Frank Chapman claimed that dubious honor. The banker-turned-ornithologist longed to see the species in the

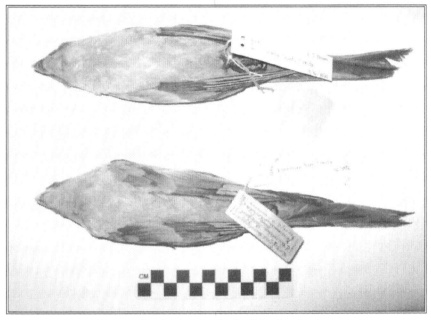

As the species neared extinction, hundreds of Carolina Parakeet specimens landed in museums. (photographed by Nathan Kraucunas, Curator of Birds and Mammals, Milwaukee Public Museum)

Doodles, a living pet Carolina Parakeet of Paul Bartsch, is shown in 1906 with a Mr. Bryan. (Courtesy of Shirley Briggs/Daniel McKinley/Christopher Cokinos)

wild; a desire fulfilled on an 1889 Florida expedition for the American Museum of Natural History. Having imagined the experience many times, Chapman, gun in hand, finally glimpsed seven parakeets on the banks of the Sebastion River. Within days, he had sighted about fifty birds in flocks numbering six to twenty. He shot several birds. One evening, Chapman contemplated the cherished specimens he had gathered. In his parakeet journal – now housed at the American Museum of Natural History in New York City – he wrote:

I admired them to my heart's content, counted them backwards and forwards[,] troubled over them generally, all the time almost doubting whether it was all true – for now we have nine specimens and I shall make no further attempt to secure others, for we have almost exterminated two of the three small flocks which occur here, and far be it from me to deal the final blows. Good luck to you poor doomed creatures, may you live to see many generations of your kind.

Two days later, Chapman reneged on his vow and shot six more parakeets. In the 1914 *Handbook of Birds of Eastern North America*, he wrote, "So far as I know, the Carolina Paroquet was last taken near Taylor Creek, northeast of Lake Okeechobee, when in April 1904, I saw thirteen and shot four."

That same year in Potter, Kansas, fruit farmer Wirt Remsburg shot a Carolina Parakeet that he mistook for a chicken hawk. The gunshot so ravaged the bird that a specimen could not be salvaged.

As extinction loomed, ornithologists and natural history collectors competed with zoos for specimens of the endangered bird. Even then, captive breeding might have saved the species; if only zoos and aviaries had cooperated in such an effort. That was not to be, however. 🐦

*The last Carolina Parakeet taken in the wild may have been shot near Taylor Creek in the Lake Okeechobee region of Florida in 1904. The bird was also rumored to have been seen in the region in 1926.
(Florida photographic Collection, Florida State Archives)*

CHAPTER FIVE

The Last Parakeet

Sometime in the 1880s, the Cincinnati Zoological Gardens paid $2.50 each for sixteen parakeets. In that shipment were Lady Jane and Incas – a pair destined to be among the last of their kind. For thirty-two years, the pair shared a cage at the Cincinnati Zoo. By 1917, they were rare birds indeed. The London Zoo offered four hundred dollars for the aging pair, even though the birds could no longer breed. The Cincinnati Zoo declined the exorbitant offer. In the summer of 1917, Lady Jane died, and Incas was left alone – a sole survivor of a once abundant species. Incas, the last Carolina Parakeet in captivity, died in 1918. An article from the February 22, 1918, *Cincinnati Times-Star* reported the loss:

A student of bird-life, acting as coroner in the case of "Incas," the Carolina parrakeet, said to be the last of its race, might enter a verdict of "died of old age." But General Manager Col. A. Stephan of the Zoo, whose study of birds goes farther [sic] than mere physical structure, development and decay knows the bird died of grief. "Incas," coveted by many zoological gardens, died Thursday night surrounded by his genuinely sorrowing friends, Col. Stephan and the keepers. Late last summer, "Lady Jane," the mate of Incas for 32 years, passed away, and after that the ancient survivor was a listless and mournful figure indeed....

The birds' passing might have been gone unnoticed by most. But surely someone missed them. Perhaps a little girl had gazed at the pair on visits to the Cincinnati Zoo's aviary. She wondered if they talked and wished she could take one home, clutch it to her breast. Maybe one day she noticed that one of the pair was gone. Her father explained

CHAPTER FIVE   *The Last Parakeet*

"*Carolina Parakeet*" watercolor by Louis Agassiz Fuertes.
(Rare and Manuscript Collections, Karl A Kroch Library, Cornell University)

that the bird died. Months later, the Carolina Parakeet exhibit was empty. When the girl asked why, her father told her of the bird's fate – that the two were the last of their kind. The zoo would replace the lost parrots with other birds, the father assured his daughter. Perhaps, she pined for the pair and her father bought a cage bird to console her. In time, the girl propably forgot Incas and Lady Jane.

The Carolina Parakeet fared no better in the wild. The last sure report of the bird in the wild was a small flock in Florida in 1920. Rumors of later sightings persisted, however. Ornithologist Charles Doe claimed to have located three pairs of parakeets in Okeechobee County, Florida in 1926. He did not collect the specimens but gathered the

Carole Boston Weatherford: THE CAROLINA PARAKEET

CHAPTER FIVE *The Last Parakeet*

"Carolina Parrot" from Animate Creation; popular edition of "Our Living World" by the Rev. J. G. Wood. Revised by Joseph B. Holder, c. 1885.

birds' eggs, instead. However, none could be positively identified. Around the same time, escaped foreign parakeets were reportedly seen in the area.

In 1934, while George Malumphy was studying wild turkeys in the Santee Swamp, he caught a glimpse of the

A young woman holds an unidentified breed of parrot, c. 1913. (Library of Congress)

supposedly-extinct ivory-billed woodpecker. He sighted the species thirty-three times, eventually arousing the curiosities of two fellow ornithologists. Alexander Sprunt, Jr., a regional supervisor for the National Audubon Society, and Herbert Stoddard visited Santee River country in search of the "extinct" ivory bill. Malumphy further enticed Sprunt and

In 1918, the last captive Carolina Parakeet died in the aviaries at the Cincinnati Zoological Gardens. (Collection of The Public Library of Cincinnati and Hamilton County)

Stoddard by claiming to have seen Carolina Parakeets on eight or nine occasions. Once, he said, seven parakeets alighted on a turkey feeding station to eat sunflower seeds.

In 1935 the National Audubon Society leased land in the area as a sanctuary and hired woodsman Warren Shokes as warden. In 1936 Sprunt and National Audubon Society sanctuary director Robert Porter Allen devised a plan to survey the swamps for the birds. From November 27 to December 3, the men visited seven baited feeding stations twice a day. On the morning of November 28, Sprunt saw a single parakeet. Five days later at dusk, he saw five more birds. Allen and Sprunt recorded several other sightings through December 11. Allen reported conclusively, "we have no hesitation in identifying these birds as Carolina Paroquets. . ."

CHAPTER FIVE — *The Last Parakeet*

No more sightings occurred until June 4, 1938 at Bluff Landing. There, Shokes spotted two adult parakeets circling and screeching overhead. Then, a young bird left the brush and flew across the creek toward an island. The older birds accompanied the youngster.

Esteemed ornithologist Ludlow Griscom later discounted Shokes' observations and disputed Allen's and Sprunt's sightings.

Nevertheless, Sprunt remained convinced of his claim. However, Allen eventually conceded that he and Sprunt probably had seen doves, not parakeets. In 1939 the habitat itself was destroyed when the land was cleared and the swamp drained to build a power plant.

By then, the American Ornithologists' Union had dismissed the Santee evidence and abandoned hope that a remnant of the species survived. The dazzling Carolina Parakeet – the only parrot native to North America – faded into extinction.

The last reported sightings of Carolina Parakeets in the wild came from the Santee Swamp in South Carolina. (Santee National Wildlife Refuge, National Fish and Wildlife Service)

CHAPTER SIX

A Perfect Likeness

The Carolina Parakeet vanished long ago from the skies and the landscape, but the bird still takes flights of fancy in the imagination. Museum-goers file past aging specimens and hand-colored lithographs. Some spectators pause and gaze at the extinct bird before them. They get a glint, perhaps even a tear, in their eyes. They are struck with a sense of what if. Even the uninitiated fall under this tiny parrot's spell.

William Powell, born in North Carolina in 1920 – too late to see a live Carolina Parakeet – stumbled across the bird's story as a youth. "My interest in the Carolina Parakeet began to develop in the late 1920s," said Powell, "when I first began to learn about it . . . and realized how narrowly I had probably missed seeing them." In subsequent years, Powell read newspaper accounts of rumored sightings. "In hopes that a report might prove true, I kept watching books and magazines," he explained. Though rumored sightings were inconclusive, Powell was smitten nonetheless. So much so, that he has devoted a lifetime to collecting images of the Carolina Parakeet. As a soldier during World War II, he acquired one of the first prints in his collection. Nearly sixty years later, he continues to search for images in libraries and bookstores and at antique shows. "In a few instances," he admits, "the frame has been more expensive than the image." Powell, a historian and professor emeritus at University of North Carolina-Chapel Hill, has numerous framed pictures of the Carolina Parakeet – some by American and others by British artists. His private gallery is a virtual aviary and

Live Carolina Parakeet (Birds of America, 1917, by T. Gilbert Pearson; courtesy of the General Library System, University of Wisconsin-Madison)

CHAPTER SIX   *A Perfect Likeness*

*"Carolina Parakeet" by Ken Gilliland.
A digital artist, Gilliland created images
of extinct, endangered and threatened
birds to raise awareness of their plight.*

shrine – testament to the fascination of birders, naturalists and artists.

A survey of price lists revealed that the Carolina Parrot is among the most expensive Audubon prints. At auction, originals range from $18,000 for a smaller royal octavo series print to $100,000 for an oversize double-elephant folio print. Reproductions start at $250 for a 1985 limited edition and approach $15,000 for a second edition. Of course, mechanically-reproduced posters cost considerably less.

The classic Carolina Parakeet print from Audubon's *Birds of America* provided reference material for a watercolor by Vince Packard, a Kent, Ohio, artist with a keen interest in the environment. "I am interested in any animal that used to live in Ohio but is now gone," said Packard. "I painted the Ivory-billed Woodpecker and did a ceramic of the Passenger Pigeon." The versatile Packard, who has painted the Carolina Parakeet at least twice, also tattooed the bird's image on an environmental lawyer.

Atlanta artist Tim Hunter, who first learned of the bird in 1998 while leafing through Audubon's *Birds of America*, has depicted the species ten times. "I see the Carolina Parakeet as an example of how mankind has attempted to subdue and exploit nature," said Hunter. His depictions of the bird range from a decorative triptych reminiscent of the French Fauves to a haunting Asian-inspired woodcut. "I am not interested in documenting or illustrating nature in a realistic manner," he said. "My work relies less on description than feeling. I would rather sum up an image as if I had seen it in passing." Of course, that perspective can only be simulated now.

Audubon and his contemporaries benefited from seeing the bird in the wild and from having freshly killed birds as subjects. Lacking formal art training, Audubon experimented with mixing media – pencil, ink, pastel, watercolor and even oils – and developed techniques to show nuances of natural colors and textures. He wired his specimens into life-like poses that gave a semblance of vitality and movement. Employing apprentices - as was common practice - to render scenic backgrounds and botanical features, Audubon set his subjects in natural habitats;

"Carolina Parakeet"
watercolor by Vince Packard
(Courtesy of the artist)

CHAPTER SIX   *A Perfect Likeness*

"Carolina Parakeets"
woodcut on paper, 30"x30,"
by Tim Hunter.
(Courtesy of the artist)

Carole Boston Weatherford: THE CAROLINA PARAKEET

*"Carolina Parakeets" casein on paper, 3
panels, 44"x90" overall, by Tim Hunter.
(Courtesy of the artist)*

CHAPTER SIX   *A Perfect Likeness*

"Carolina Parakeets and Orchids"
oil painting by Sandra Baggette
(Courtesy of the artist)

thus harmonizing the background and foreground, the bird and its environment. This pioneering approach achieved an unprecedented degree of realism. Prior to Audubon, most wildlife artists rendered birds in stiff profile as if stuffed and mounted in museum cases. In contrast, Aububon's watercolors and engravings of Carolina Parakeets seem to capture moments in nature.

Indeed, he was in the right place at the right time. Born in 1785 in present-day Haiti to a French sea captain and plantation owner and his mulatto mistress, Audubon was just four years old when his mother died. He was raised in France, where he cultivated an appreciation for art, music and nature. In 1808 at age eighteen, Audubon was sent to his father's Mill Grove estate near Philadelphia. For the French emigré, the move would prove to be fortuitous. At the family estate, he studied, hunted and took up birding as a hobby. He also conducted the continent's first-known bird banding. By tying strings around the legs of Eastern Phoebes, he learned that the bird returned annually to the same nesting sites.

After more than a decade in a dry goods business in Kentucky, Audubon, then bankrupt, began an epic quest to document America's avifauna. In the wilds, he lived a rugged hand-to-mouth existence that tested both strength and endurance. The sacrifice paid off, however. His seminal work, *The Birds of America*, was published from 1827 to 1838. The oversize portfolio of 435 copper-engraved and hand-colored plates of birds created a sensation. Riding the crest of American romanticism, Audubon became the country's leading wildlife artist. And his work became the standard by which all others would be measured. But even as he captured the young nation's sublime beauty, vast landscapes – and teeming flocks in the skies above – were virtually disappearing before his eyes.

These days, depicting the extinct Carolina Parakeet poses challenges. In 2001, wildlife artist Marc Bohan completed a watercolor of a single Carolina Parakeet. "Reference material was hard to come by," said

"Carolina Parakeets" sculpture by Grainger McKoy, 1992. Basswood, alabaster, steel and oil paint. (Collection of Dan W. Lufkin)

CHAPTER SIX   *A Perfect Likeness*

Bohan, who has painted several extinct birds. "This painting is based on a stuffed specimen at Michigan State University's museum and photos of related parrots. Since most specimens are over a hundred years old, they are typically dusty and faded." For Bohan, the painting amounted to a mission: "[T]o make a lifelike, accurate representative of its species, [that allows] the viewer to connect with the bird as an individual personality [and] realize what they have lost."

South Carolina painter Sandra Baggette first heard of the Carolina Parakeet in the 1980s. But she hesitated to paint the species. "I usually paint from life or my photos or sketches," said Baggette. "I had trouble finding enough material to paint the bird." Gradually, written descriptions and other artists' renderings helped her conjure her own vision of the bird. In 2001, Baggette decided to pair a caged Carolina Parakeet with an orchid. "Both are treasures," she said.

In 2002, the South Carolina Governor's office tapped painter Tyrone Geter to craft a Christmas ornament representing a bird native to the state. Getter, a professor and gallery director at Benedict College in Columbia, South Carolina, selected the Carolina Parakeet specifically because it was extinct. With wire, papier-mache and vivid color, he depicted the bird coming in for a landing. Geter's Carolina Parakeet adorned an eighteen-foot noble fir, the official White House Christmas tree.

South Carolina sculptor Grainger McKoy also rendered the Carolina Parakeet in flight. Inspired by ornithologist Alexander Wilson's ninteenth century account of the birds in *American Ornithology*, McKoy carved a flock of five parakeets in wild descent. McKoy's basswood, albaster and steel sculpture recreates Wilson's observation of the birds "in the month of February, along the banks of the Ohio, in a snow storm, flyng about like pigeons, in full cry."

"I read that and saw the whole carving," said McKoy, whose startlingly life-like sculptures are reminiscent of videotape freeze-frames. Early in his career, the artist helped refine the technique of detailing and inserting wooden feathers. He also pioneered techniques for carving birds in

CHAPTER SIX

A Perfect Likeness

flight. Defying both gravity and belief, his compositions not only elevate bird carving from craft to art but achieve extraordinary realism that evokes natural habitats.

"Imagine being an Indian," said McKoy, "down in the swamp at first light, hunting deer, and that sycamore you're leaning against starts to wake up, comes to life inside, and you look up just in time to see a flock of parakeets swirling out of the top."

Thomas A. Bennett, the first artist-in-residence at the North Carolina Museum of Natural Sciences in Raleigh, began drawing birds when he was just five years old. His initial subject: a wild turkey. A couple years later, his grandfather told him a story that made a lasting impression. "When he was a little boy himself on a farm in Osceola County, Florida," said Bennett of his grandfather, "the Carolina Parakeet would come in large flocks and alight on the mulberry trees."

In 1999 Bennett – whose work is reminiscent of Audubon's – began a series on the natural history of the Carolinas with a painting of the Carolina Parakeet. The masterful work, rendered in a 19th century vignette style, shows five birds on a moss-draped cypress – a quintessential Low Country backdrop.

Yet, Bennett's painting can not possibly do justice to the species that inspired it. For the Carolina Parakeet, there is no justice. And there will be no resurrection. "The loss ... is to me unbelievable," said Bennett. "People don't realize how fragile our environment is."

Or how tenuous a species can be. Today, we can behold wildlife art and view stuffed, mounted birds. But we will never again see the Carolina Parakeet grace the skies. At natural history museums, we can only gaze at glass-enclosed specimens and sigh. 🌎

The Carolina Parakeet's Former Range

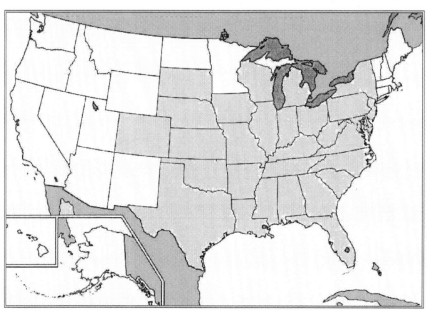

East Coast and Gulf States
Alabama
Delaware
Florida
Georgia
Louisiana
Maryland
Mississippi
New Jersey
New York
North Carolina
Pennsylvania
South Carolina
Texas
Virginia
Washington, D.C.

Mississippi Valley and tributaries
Arkansas
Colorado
Illinois
Indiana
Iowa
Kansas
Kentucky
Michigan
Missouri
Nebraska
Ohio
Oklahoma
South Dakota
Tennessee
West Virginia
Wisconsin

Note:
This list combines data from documented sightings, anecdotal historical reports and contemporary bird checklists.

Courtesy of www.larvalbug.com

A Partial Listing of Museums Exhibiting Carolina Parakeet Specimens

American Museum of
Natural History,
New York, New York

American Philosophical Society,
Philadelphia, Pennsylvania

Anniston Museum of
Natural History,
Anniston, Alabama

Carnegie Museum of
Natural History,
Pittsburgh, Pennsylvania

Chicago Academy of Sciences
Nature Museum,
Chicago, Illinois

Denver Museum of
Nature and Science,
Denver, Colorado

Field Museum of
Natural History,
Chicago, Illinois

Harvard Museum of
Natural History,
Cambridge, Massachusetts

Museum of Natural Science,
Louisiana State University,
Baton Rouge, Louisiana

North Carolina Museum of
Natural Sciences,
Raleigh, North Carolina

University of Iowa
Museum of Natural History,
Iowa City, Iowa

Bibliography

Audubon, John James.
The Birds of America.
New York: Macmillan, 1941.

Audubon, John James.
Original Watercolors by John James Audubon for The Birds of America.
New York: American Heritage/Bonanza Books, 1985.

Audubon, John James.
Writings and Drawings.
New York: Library of America, 1999, 233-37.

Baird, S. F.; Brewer, T. M.; and Ridgway, R.
A History of North American Birds: Land Birds, Vol. 2.
Boston: Little Brown, and Company, 1874.

Bendire, Charles.
Life Histories of North American Birds.
Washington: Government Printing Office, 1892.

Bartsch, Paul.
"A Pet Carolina Paroquet."
The Bird Watchers Anthology.
Edited by Roger Tory Peterson.
New York: Harcourt, Brace and Company, 1957, 148-151.

Burleigh, Robert;
ill. by Wendell Minor.
Into the Woods: John James Audubon Lives His Dream.
New York: Atheneum, 2003.

"Carolina Parakeets,"
Discovering Lewis & Clark.
<http://lewis-clark.org/FREEMANCUSTIS/ILLUS-E/bi-caroparaE.htm>
(February 28, 2003).

Catesby, Mark.
Natural History of Carolina, Florida, and the Bahama Islands:
Containing the Figure of Birds, Beasts, Fishes, Serpents, Insects, and Plants. . . London: White, 1771.

Chapman, Frank.
Handbook of Eastern North American Birds. New York: D. Appleton and Company, 1914.

Cokinos, Christopher.
Hope Is the Thing with Feathers: A Personal Chronicle of Vanished Birds.
New York: Jeremy P. Tarcher/Putnam, 2000, 7-58.

Feduccia, Alan, ed.
Catesby's Birds of Colonial America.
Chapel Hill:
University of North Carolina Press, 1985, 64-66.

**Forshaw, Joseph;
Howell, Steve;
Lindsey, Terrence; and
Stallcup, Rich.**
A Nature Company Guide to Birding.
San Francisco: Time-Life Books, 1994, 80-81.

Fuller, Errol.
Extinct Birds.
New York: Facts on File Publications, 1987, 150-53.

Grosvenor, Gilbert, ed.
The Book of Birds. Washington: National Geographic Society, 1937, 80.

Hasbrouck, Edwin M.
"The Carolina Paroquet."
Thge Auk 8 (October 1891): 368-379).

"History of Santee Cooper."
Santee Cooper Power Project.
<http://www.santeecooper.com/aboutus/history.html>
(March 24, 2003).

Laycock, George.
"The Last Parakeet."
Audubon 71 (March 1969): 21-25.

"Lewis and Clark:
The Archives. The Journals"
Public Broadcasting Service.
<www.pbs.org/lewisandclark/archive/journal.html>
(February 28, 2003).

Martin, Margaret.
A Long Look at Nature: The North Carolina Museum of Natural Sciences.
Chapel Hill: University of North Carolina Press, 2001, 111-12.

McKinley, Daniel.
"The Carolina Parakeet in Pioneer Misourri."
The Wilson Bulletin 72, 3 (September 1960), 275-290.

BIBLIOGRAPHY

Nickens, T. Edward.
"For the Birds."
Carolina Alumni Review 91, 6 (November-December 2002): 50-58.

Nowotny, Dr.
"The Breeding of the Carolina Paroquet in Captivity."
The Auk 15 (January 1898): 28-32.

Nuttall, Thomas.
A Manual of the Ornithology of the United States and Canada: The Land Birds.
Boston: Hilliard, Gray and Company, 1814, 646-651.

Pearson, Thomas Gilbert; Brimley, Clement Samuel; and Brimley, Herbert Hutchinson.
Birds of North Carolina.
Raleigh: North Carolina Department of Agriculture, State Museum Division, 1959, 205.

Saikku, Mikko.
"The Extinction of the Carolina Parakeet."
Environmental History Review (Fall 1990): 2-18.

Snyder, Noel F. R., and **Russell, Keith.**
"Carolina Parakeet."
The Birds of North America 667 (2002).

Studer, Jacob.
The Birds of North America.
New York: Harrison House, 1977
(fascimile of 1881 edition).

Thomas, Cornelius M. D. James Forte,
a 17th century settelment, possibly, pre-1625, from the earliest known map of the Cape Fear River, the John Locke sketch of the Shapley map of the Cape Fear River, 1662, together with the Lancaster map of the Cape Fear River, 1679, and the Hilton pamphlet, printed from originals. An enigma presented in booklet form. Wilmington, N.C.: J.E. Hicks for Charles Towne Preservation Trust, 1959, 25-26.

Williams, Buzz.
"Passenger Pigeon and Carolina Parakeet: Vanished Birds." *The Chattooga Quarterly* (Spring 2000). <http://www.chattoogariver.org/Articles/2000S/Birds.htm.>. (March 13, 2003).

Wilson, Alexander.
American Ornithology. Philadelphia: Bradford & Inskeep. 1808-1814.

Bibliography

An award-winning poet and author, Carole Boston Weatherford is the author of eighteen books of poetry, nonfiction and children's literature. Her poetry for adults is collected in *Stormy Blues*, and the prize-winning chapbooks *The Tar Baby on the Soapbox* and *The Tan Chanteuse*. Her nonfiction titles include *A Negro League Scrapbook* and *Sink or Swim: African-American Lifesavers of the Outer Banks*. Her picture book *The Sound That Jazz Makes* won the Carter G. Woodson Award from National Council for the Social Studies and an NAACP Image Award nomination. Her poetry collection, *Remember the Bridge: Poems of a People*, won the North Carolina Juvenile Literature Award and the International Reading Associationís Teacherís Choice Award. She is Distinguished Visiting Professor at Fayetteville State University. She resides in High Point, N.C., with her husband and their two children.

www.caroleweatherford.com

Made in the USA
Lexington, KY
15 January 2010